Cure Violence

Cure Violence

STOP
Bullying

and You'll Stop Gun Violence

by Anthony Montgomery

MILL CITY PRESS

Mill City Press, Inc.
2301 Lucien Way #415
Maitland, FL 32751
407.339.4217
www.millcitypress.net

Printed in the United States of America

Library of Congress Control Number: 2020911602

Paperback ISBN-13: 978-1-6312-9719-9
Ebook ISBN-13: 978-1-6312-9720-5

Chapter One

C razy, out of control, people are near you – every day. Some of them are a ticking time bomb, ready to explode any minute. Do you work in a large city? Look around... see that guy? He's the one who's *not* heading to an office. He has nowhere to go; he's hunting. Don't talk to him – don't engage him. Especially, don't make eye contact. Leave him *alone*. He could really ruin your day.

Maybe you live in a rural area or small town, and you think you're safe. Nope, you're still not exempt from violence.

If you don't take this scenario seriously, I have credibility. I know what I'm talking about – I used to be one of those people with an explosive temperament. I belonged, as so many do, to a gang.

It doesn't take much to set someone off. Maybe they got up that morning and just decided it was a good day to kill someone... anyone, *it doesn't matter who*. That's his plan for the day, and you don't want to be the unlucky person to land on his radar.

A person who is always alone, always lonely, is the most dangerous person you'll ever meet. He or she is quiet, but planning... planning *something* that you don't want to be around for. He is deadly serious and won't hesitate for a second before ending a stranger's life. He might have a new gun that needs testing out. Or he might wake up and just feel like killing. Find a person and – in street slang – *catch a body*.

There is so much violence – especially gun violence – in our world today.

This kind of extreme violence doesn't just randomly occur in a well-balanced person and cause them to strike out at random strangers. That kind of anger has to brew and simmer for years before exploding. I think it all stems from bullying.

I believe that if we can end bullying, we can end the fury, the cruelty, the destructiveness, the loss of human lives – lives of people who are loved by others.

When I say "bullying," I'm saying a lot. I mean everything that involves one person or group selecting a victim and picking on him or her. Bullying includes in-person teasing, harassing, cyberbullying, rape, incest, battering or physical abuse, mental abuse, racism, intimidation, making threats, stalking, and any type of assault, verbal or physical that violates the personal boundaries or free will of an individual. Family-based mistreatment includes either one-time or ongoing, harsh taunting, insulting, or ridiculing.

But, a massive amount of anger stems from childhood. Parents often neglect their children. They could be living at their wit's end, trying to survive financially. They probably had no positive role models to help them learn how to be a good parent. As a child, they may have been the one who everyone picked on.

It doesn't take much for kids to find a victim. It's usually someone who stands out as different. *The stupid one. The ugly one.* The fat one, the one with freckles, or the disabled one. You got harassed because you were the black kid or the only Hispanic kid. Or any reason a kid is different.

Parents who struggle may have been the one who got smacked around more than every other kid in the family. Or was bullied in school. They grew up and didn't heal. They're still that kid who feels inferior; they're the one who is tensed, waiting for an ambush. They may be in a relationship with someone who provides that expected beating.

Someone has to step up and decide to break generational curses that allow problems to continue through each generation of new family members. Someone has to decide to *not abuse* or neglect their children. They need to learn how to raise children who believe in their self-worth, children who can grow up without anger and resentment festering in their soul.

With so many broken families, you can lose your family identity. Young kids see their families struggling, fighting, scrabbling for their next meal. It scares kids; they've lost any security they ever had. There might be an aunt who's constantly fighting with a cousin, doing each other wrong, calling child welfare on the other one, making false reports, talking bad, even making violent threats – anger taken to the point of death threats. These altercations usually happen in front of the whole family, mostly because people become loud, and it draws a crowd. After someone stomps off, anger builds, each side believing they're right.

Family identity is broken even further. Now, the kids are basically dead to part of the family; grudges can be held for years. And a lot of people don't really have too much family to start with.

Sibling rivalry plays a big part of the problem. Just because we may be brother and sister does not mean we grew up the same. When the mom has different baby-fathers, or when parents pick one child as their favorite, this becomes a problem and will lead to many other problems.

For instance, a woman has two children with a man. Maybe he ends up going to prison. Then, she moves on to another guy. She has a baby with him, now she has children from different fathers. She may be drawn more to the newer baby because she's still *with* the father. She sees that baby as representing love with her current man and could subconsciously resent the other children for reminding her of a man that she's no longer romantically involved with. That resentment can increase if he'd ever cheated on her or beat her. Those kids suffer even though they've done nothing wrong. They can be used as a punching bag or be on the receiving end of verbal abuse as a parent takes out their anger on their children.

Understand something. When you go through a traumatic situation, whether you have killed someone or you've witnessed other people being killed, *you're affected*. If you've been imprisoned, lived in a shelter, group home, on the street, been put into a drug rehab center, mental hospital, or sick ward, it's gonna change you. That trauma is going to affect you long-term. You could end up in a very dark place. Some of your friends may even choose not to hang around with you anymore.

By changing behavior, by actively loving the people around you, you can break that generational curse of abuse. Realize what you're doing when you tell your child that they're no good. Or that they're just like their deadbeat father and will never amount to anything. Try – one day at a time – to show love and appreciation to your family. Work together. Eat meals together. Talk to each other. Focus on the *positive*. Unlearn negative behavior and hurtful phrases you've said to others in the past. Build a better life together, one step, one positive statement, one hug at a time.

Chapter Two

Racism is a form of bullying.

Displaying prejudice, discrimination, or antagonism against someone of a different race is racism in a nutshell. It's based on the negative beliefs and actions taken by a person and inflicted on another. People who routinely tell jokes that make fun of an entire race are expressing their hatred, couched in the form of humor. "He didn't mean nuthin' by it" is the usual way of rationalizing such offensive and blatant racism. Those who openly demonstrate this behavior generally live with the confidence that their race is superior to another.

It's nearly impossible to change the mind of adults with fully-rooted beliefs that others are inferior. They've grown up like that. It's a *learned behavior*, not something found in genetics. Parents subtly influence their children, as they grow, to acquire tastes (such as with food, activities, lifestyle, and language) similar to the family's preferences. They also pass on hurtful attitudes and behavior about people who are different than themselves, often displaying zero tolerance for any diversity. It's a mindset meant to dehumanize people. Those people are targets. A racist person has been trained, since childhood, to realize others are inferior. A short-list includes black people, Hispanic, Asian, Native Americans, and LGBTQ – although not a race, the community of gay, lesbian, trans people are included in any list regarding bullying. They are frequent recipients of hate crimes.

Now, many people ask, *What about racism toward white people?* There is no such thing, and here's why.

White people can be treated with prejudice, but it's not true racist behavior. With white people's racist views toward people of color, racist attitudes, behavior, and mindset are *systemic*. It shows up in every facet of our lives, from hiring practices to race-based gaps in income, local and federal incarceration, government surveillance, drug arrests, and housing discrimination. It shows up in one person's ability to walk into a small store versus another person – who happens to be a person of color. Some people automatically react with fear, anger, resentment, or hatred, depending on who they are and how they were raised.

Racism also becomes bullying. Look at the statistics; Hispanic, Native American, Middle-Eastern, African-American people are commonly treated with attitudes of disrespect, letting the person know they *just don't fit in here*. If your name is a white-sounding name (Robert O'Sullivan), you are twice as likely to get a callback from a job application than if your name is DeShawn Jackson or LaKeisha Brown. People who control others use their power to surround themselves with others similar to themselves. That's a form of bullying.

Racism is police treating people of color differently than they treat Caucasians with a European heritage. Black people are more likely to be pulled over, arrested, and incarcerated. People argue that black people commit more crimes. I don't believe it can be as simple as that. Black people have fewer opportunities and zero white privilege, so it only makes sense that they will turn to crime to try and improve their lives. Or at least numb the pain of their daily existence.

Many people of color who live in low-income areas experience zero to low upward economic mobility due to limited access to quality schools, safe neighborhoods, reliable transportation, or better-paying jobs. Their lives become a glass ceiling. Sometimes, practical methods are implemented in more affluent communities, such as refusing to accept rent-assistance vouchers. This is one way to prevent low-income families from moving into these communities and taking a step up toward improving their living conditions and lifestyle.

Institutional or commercial policies that exclude African-Americans from predominately white neighborhoods, while simultaneously disinvesting in black communities has kept better schools and higher-paying jobs out of their reach. Then, people condemn them as a whole for not achieving as much success in their education, employment, or acquiring material possessions as an average white person.

By limiting the achievable goals of people as a whole, it causes a build-up of frustration, anger, dissatisfaction, and hopelessness. You now have a ticking time bomb.

That time bomb had its beginning, most likely, in the beginning. If a teen girl becomes pregnant, she's not emotionally prepared to handle a baby. If the boy and girl decide to marry, the boy is not emotionally prepared to handle family life. He doesn't have any training on how to care for an infant. Too many times, resentment brews and spills over into an argument. That escalates into someone stomping out, or possibly physical aggression. The baby is in the middle of this. Maybe he or she only needs a diaper changed. Maybe she needs feeding. An infant has only one method of communication when she has a problem. She cries. If she is regularly neglected, that's a form of bullying. She grows up, realizing, "You're picking on me."

Whatever reason an infant started crying, she will hear the arguments, raised voices, and feel the stress. The baby, after screaming begins, will certainly need comforting. However, neither parent is in a state to gentle their emotions enough to provide a calm, quiet, and soothing atmosphere.

In the blink of an eye, the unthinkable happens. Someone grabs the baby and shakes her, screaming, "Stop it!" In as little as five seconds of shaking, the baby can suffer from bruising and bleeding in the brain, brain swelling, spinal cord injury, and other irreversible problems, including death.

If a baby does not permanently suffer physical injury, in a dysfunctional setting, he will go on to experience possible emotional abuse, develop a lack of self-esteem, and grow up learning that anger and violence are a normal part of life.

Children in dysfunctional homes live with a plethora of difficult situations. The following is a list of things children have to worry about, protect themselves from, or deal with every day.

- Witnessing police brutality
- School bullying
- Neighborhood gangs
- Family (or later personal) incarceration

- Broken families (an ever-changing family dynamic leaves children living on shifting sand instead of solid ground.)
- Sibling rivalry (It can be worse if children are from different fathers/mothers. One child's parent can treat them better than the other children's parents, causing jealousy, anger, resentment.)
- Racism, hate crimes
- Immigration, fear of deportation for many living in America. Possibly forced to live sequestered away from prying eyes.
- Confusion over sexual orientation
- Problems in the home, such as extra relatives living together, resulting in not enough food or beds.
- STD, children can either be born with it or acquire it through teen sexual activity.
- Pregnancy
- Rape or molestation from family members or others living in the same home or visiting regularly.

Adults are not exempt from daily worries. Those who live with unstable homes or a poor financial situation will experience a greater amount of issues to stress over.

- Job safety
- The boss fires you for no reason, and you've got no protection or savings to fall back on.
- Marriage – is he/she the right one? Will they cheat on me? Will they be good to my children?

- The single life – living on one income, worry over finding a good, compatible mate.
- Raising children, feeding them, the expense of clothing, education.
- Life insurance, can't afford it, but not responsible to live without it.
- Health insurance. Many working poor either have no health insurance, or employers provide a high deductible, catastrophic plan.
- Handicapped or disabled individuals have an extra burden of living with lessened abilities as compared to healthy people. They frequently live on government-assisted income and have limited prescription insurance. If they can work part-time, they may actually be in a worse situation, such as being ineligible for assistance or other state or federal programs.
- Having a police record limits people in many ways. Poor choices made in early adult years create a record that will follow them forever, lowering the odds of getting a good job. Employers can take into account arrests and convictions.
- Many people live with in-law problems. They can be ongoing conflict and cause regular arguments, discord, and even police intervention.
- One in every four women and one in every nine men experience severe partner physical violence, sexual violence, or stalking. They can suffer from injury from slapping or shoving, living with fear, post-traumatic stress disorder, or contraction of an STD.
- Partners can suffer from sex issues. One person may desire a more frequent or varied sexual

relationship, so cheating can happen. They may be sexually incompatible, or if one is considered not good in bed, their partner could cheat.

Chapter Three

Walk with me. Let's talk.

You say you want to stop youth violence. From the federal government to cities and small towns, all Americans play a part in this. We all sit around and shake our heads, wondering what causes all the crime, seemingly random killings, mass murders in crowds. Here's a clue: it is not violent video games or movies.

It starts with bullying. It starts with attitudes. It starts by making fun of people, and picking on their weak points. Most of the people around you are only there for themselves and not to help. America needs to band together to end rivalry among races, among political parties, between genders, and especially between family members.

It's not a contest to see who is better than the next person. Here's an insider scoop: *we're all the same. No one is better. There will always be people who are prettier, richer, or more successful – but those qualities do not affect human worth.*

There's only one race – the human race.

We all want the same things. We all want love, acceptance, success, pride, a sense of accomplishment, security and safety, and the qualities that a home brings: food, water, warmth, and rest in an environment of support and freedom from fear.

There are so many households where a woman and man are living, but not in a healthy relationship. Many times, a man is only looking for personal survival. So, he lies to a woman who has a home, kids, and maybe low self-esteem. "I love you, baby," he says. What he means is, "I don't got no job. I got myself all set up right here, nice and comfy. No way am I going onto the street and have nothing." So, he stays put, pretending he cares about the woman and her kids until something better comes along. In a dysfunctional relationship, his frustration and anger will eventually seep out; he'll lose control and take it out on the woman or her child. Then, it will become a habit. He was probably teased, picked on, abused, or molested as a child. Living with daily anxiety from his past could be part of the reason why he doesn't have a job. It may be why he's seen the inside of jail or prison. He knows he's been picked on, bullied, or abused, but doesn't know how to resolve the emotions he feels. Childhood trauma can result in an adult with problems in every area of his life, such as emotional health, mental health, physical health, and relationships. The distress will spill over into a person's work life, affecting his ability to get along with co-workers and authority, and resulting in an inability to maintain a long-term job.

To combat stress, people often self-medicate with different types of *medicines*. Those under pressure don't seek out the professional help they need. They turn to drugs or alcohol most often. They need to numb the internal pain. It doesn't matter if you use Tylenol, tequila, or beer. They have the same results when taking care of pain – depending on whether you have a physical headache or live with memories of decades of abuse.

People don't adjust all by themselves; there is no counseling for these extreme types of problems. The anger in people will eventually cause them to explode. They're living on the verge of "I can't take no more." They're looking for respect. They're looking for a place to belong. They're looking for people who have an unleashed anger building inside. They get caught up in a gang and *bam!* They're a soldier.

When a person experiences more pain than they can bear, their frustration builds. Then, they get backed into a corner and can't run anymore. It becomes a do-or-die situation. He starts hurting people because he can't see any tomorrow. There's no relief in sight. He has no hope, only pain. In his mind, there is no such thing as an innocent person, maybe you *personally* didn't do anything, but someone you know may have. You or your family will pay the price.

Gangs have a habit of killing each other to gain power. They bring in money through drug sales, extortion, and many other crimes and immoral activities. To indoctrinate new members, they play on the weaknesses of younger people. If you have a broken family, gangs offer a place to belong, where you can be respected, have power, and belong. If you don't see a college education and good job prospects in your future, you can join a gang, be protected, and earn lucrative amounts of money by selling drugs or other illegal activity. You will carry a gun. *You will use it.*

I was born into a gang. I lived in the projects in the Bronx, in New York. The building my family lived in was part of the territory of the Zulu Nation. They were part of a larger gang. As I grew up, I began assuming an active part of the Zulu Nation. I was in elementary school. A gang is much like quicksand, it looks calm and smooth from far off, but get close enough, and you'll get sucked in.

Eventually, I became a leader. I had two-hundred-plus soldiers. Back then, we used pagers to contact each other. Nobody had cell phones. We used pay phones and input codes in so you knew who it was. It was an early form of caller I.D. As the leader, it was my responsibility to ensure the gang's survival, to provide food when necessary, and make sure everyone was respected. The soldiers depend on their leader. I provided protection, guidance, and income for my soldiers. If someone was homeless, I could offer them a place to sleep. If they were hungry, they dropped by for a little something. Being a leader was a full-time job; I didn't work at a normal job.

If you can't take care of the people under you, then why are you trying to build something? If a member from another gang came over to sell drugs in our territory, we made them pay protection money for encroaching on our area.

To be a successful gang, you need street-ability – *pull* on the streets, *connections*. People in my clique came over to my apartment to hang out. But, my attitude was, *If you ain't down with me, don't come around.* Don't come around if you don't join. You can't come and see and listen to what's going down, then leave. I'm gonna take you for a snitch for the police or another organization. Other gangs want to find out what's happening and then move in on you.

A person with power has strength. In his own territory, he can do what he wants. For example, a *soldier* – part of the local clique – is walking in town and sees a couple, a husband and wife. The woman is fine-looking. So as he walks past, he smacks the woman's butt. Now, the soldier knows that the husband, who looks like he works in an office, is no match for him and is powerless in a fight. The husband knows this also, so does not engage him, but says, "I'm going to call 911." That's about the worst thing he can do. The soldier won't hesitate to hurt him, take him down. He won't risk letting a guy call the police. The soldier showed him that there's nothing the husband can do; he's powerless, and that's the point. The wife feels disrespected and possibly disappointed in her man. If the husband backs down, the soldier walks on, having displayed his power. The husband's choice is to live with feelings of cowardice or die.

Chapter Four

Anyone who's never been involved in any street life like a gang may ask why these people don't go to counseling and resolve their emotional problems. That's a nice thought, but, in this case, it's unrealistic. I've never heard of a counselor who went through anything like gang life. If you didn't walk through something, you have no idea what your patient is talking about.

Long ago, a female told me how she'd been raped. She'd previously talked about it to another woman, who said, "You need to just get over it."

The violated female asked her, "How can I get over it? He messed me up. He didn't stop after the first time – he raped me three times. *He broke me*." Her girlfriend had never experienced anything like that, so how could she really understand how her friend reacted?

Women play a big part in an organization. Sometimes they fight, and sometimes they're used in another way. A woman gives sex to a man from a rival gang. In his vulnerable state, she gets information from him. The next thing you know, he's hanging from a tree.

In gangs, outside of gangs, there's sexual harassment. It happens. It's real. You just aren't seeing it for what it is. While I was in the Zulu gang, I heard of a twist on sexual harassment. A woman who was a lesbian and a clique leader. She had a crush on a woman who didn't reciprocate her feelings. After hearing "No" enough times, the leader repeatedly went to the woman's place of employment and harassed her. She was able to cause enough disruption so the woman was on the verge of losing her job.

That situation demonstrated that the leader had enough clout to get what she wanted. I say this not to disrespect lesbians, and this is not typical behavior among any group or community. This is just relating a story to show how gang mentality builds on the idea that you can gain power, move up through the ranks, and exert power and control over other people.

Sexual harassment happens everywhere, not just in the workplace. Some examples of inappropriate behavior include:

- Repeatedly making compliments of someone's appearance
- Discussing sex in front of others
- Smacking another's butt
- Touching another's arm and lingering too long. Also any form of fondling
- Distributing nude photos or photos of women or men
- Telling sexual jokes or any innuendo that makes someone uncomfortable
- Sending or forwarding sexually suggestive text messages or emails
- Whistling or catcalling in public
- Gossiping to relate rumors about someone's sex life
- Repeatedly embracing, hugging or other unwanted touching

- Of course, rape and molestation
- Any word, look, or act that makes someone uncomfortable

Sexual harassment isn't restricted to a man offending a woman. It can be woman/woman, man/man, man/woman. It can be overt or quite subtle, leaving the victim questioning the other's intent.

There is violence in every generation. I saw racist attituded between black people, Puerto Ricans, and Hispanics, each having their own gangs. When people think they're better than another race, there's going to be conflict. You feel disrespected and will fight back.

For instance, when you walk too close to a wild animal, they get nervous and upset. Push them – they'll react. Everybody has an animalistic instinct inside. Each person has their own breaking point, and it could be different every day. They get fed up and lose their temper. *Snap*. Someone is dead. There are so many people in jail, saying, "I don't even know what happened." They weren't thinking. They didn't plan it. It just happened – they killed someone, possibly a stranger. But in the heat of the moment, they acted. If they were carrying, they could have used a knife, a gun to kill, or maybe they were just a better fighter.

Some people live on the edge. Others are that ticking time bomb. All it might take is for you to glance at him – make eye contact and you're the target. If he can't get to you, he'll take out your family.

If you see a person staring at you, you're his target. You may resemble someone who hurt him once. Anger is commonly deflected to another person. Especially if they can't take revenge on the one who bullied, picked on, controlled, or abused him. Or her.

People who control others have power. Manipulation is a commonly used tool. Force is used in the blink of an eye. Drug dealers, once they've established themselves and have power, they develop an attitude like: *You can't beat me, so I'm going to take over your house, kick you out, and start selling drugs from there.*

People don't take things seriously. Parents, learn to back off if you're picking on your kids. Figure it out. Don't act like the kids are the reason your life is miserable.

If you push the wrong person, you get the guns. Like, full *4th of July fireworks* come out. Big guns.

Possible reasons for a school shooting, drive-by, or house shot up? Sometimes, if they can't get to you, they're gonna take out someone else. Like, "You did me wrong, so I'm gonna rape your sister." "I'm gonna shoot your kid at school."

When on-the-edge people shoot to kill, maybe it's because "I gonna test out a new gun. Someone gotta go."

Or maybe they just woke up that day and had a gut feeling of, "I gotta shoot a body." He doesn't care. He knows it's gonna make a family cry – that's what he wants, to see them suffer. Somehow it makes him feel better that someone else is in pain. "If I'm in pain, somebody else gonna be in pain. If i gotta cry, some else gonna cry."

Chapter Five

When people have nowhere to turn to belong, to be respected, to stop being invisible or bullied, they need to create a new family because theirs is broken. They get into a gang, the one in their neighborhood.

Kids are growing up without knowing how to become an adult. They don't know how to show love or physical contact – other than sex. They don't have any hope for the future.

We, as Americans, need to put programs in place to help people teach teens practical things, like how to fill out a job application, how to cook food, how to take care of babies. We should be teaching responsibility with finances, how to spend time with children, and how to be a good parent, an involved, caring parent. They need to know how to put their past behind them and not continue generational curses that perpetuate abuse, alcoholism, drug abuse, poverty, lack of education. They need to learn how to redirect anger and not take it out on others. They need to learn how not to be violent.

Adults and parents are also living maladjusted lives. Maybe they don't know how to cook and relay on a food bank or EBT to buy frozen easy to heat meals. That isn't healthy, and it's much more expensive. Adults need to be taught the same things as the kids – how to be financially responsible, how to fill out a job application, how to cook nutritious and filling meals. They need help with figuring out how to build a better life.

This can't happen overnight. It needs to be taught, one day at a time. It needs to be put into practice by adults and young adults. Practice love.

Everyone has some degree of power. You can use your power for good or evil. I advocate using your power, your energy, your influence to help your community become better and more prosperous.

In my mid-twenties, I retired from Zulu, passed leadership to my cousin. I started my own organization. But, this time, instead of extortion and drugs, I focused on helping the community. I wanted to put back into my neighborhood what we had taken out. I made it a priority to create positive benefits. One way was by helping kids direct their energy on healthy, beneficial activities.

A few of the important concepts that people – kids, teens, and adults – need to learn are:

- Teach and learn respect. Respect for yourself and for others.
- Teach that everyone has got something wrong with them. You just can't always see it. Or maybe someone in your family has something wrong with them. Everyone thinks they're normal, but what if you're handicapped with poor math or reading skills? You could have impaired cognitive ability. You might have a food allergy or IBS (Irritable Bowel Syndrome) which, if undiagnosed and untreated, can make your life miserable.

- Teach people to stop gossiping. It's harmful. It's mean. I know that men do it but in my experience, mostly females like to gossip. And it's not always the truth. Probably, it's rarely the truth being told. Everybody wants to be better than other people, so teach kids young that they're really not *better*. Teach them to help instead of tearing down others.

- It's gotta be in you to stop doing what you don't want to do. Some people are ignorant. You can't change somebody who doesn't want to change or is just too stupid to grasp that helping others brings a greater joy and satisfaction. Hurting others may bring a temporary elation, but it will not bring anyone long-term happiness.

- People know what they're doing. They know they're causing pain and misery. They get older and play stupid on purpose because they don't want to change. They think like, "You're gonna keep doing what I don't like, so I'm going to go whack you upside your head." They like to start something and then play hurt. They are the ones who continually stir the pot, keep things going, keep people in contention.

- Learn to see eye-to-eye with people. You're not always gonna be right, so be open to different ideas.

- Listen. This is important. Some people don't listen, they just wait for you to stop talking so they can. When you reach the point of, "If you don't want to hear my side, I'm not going to listen to you," brick walls come up. People retaliate with violence or other ways to hurt you.

- Sticks and stones can break my bones, but words can never hurt me. That's the biggest lie ever told. *Words do hurt*. When you tell someone, especially a child, that they're worthless or stupid or "I wish you'd never been born," those words stay inside them forever.

Conclusion

I believe that if everyone helps, looks back, and offers a helping hand to those you left behind, we can make the world better. We can end the violence if everyone works together.

Below are some resources that can help. Please use them. I hope for you a better life than you have had. I hope for you to achieve better attitudes, better relationships, better nutrition in your daily life, and better education and employment opportunities. If you work toward a happier, less abrasive lifestyle, you'll conquer the pain and live with peace.

https://www.stopbullying.gov/ On this website, they give you tools to help prevent bullying, organize community events, and how to recognize the signs of bullying.

https://www.consumer.ftc.gov/topics/protecting-kids-online This website focuses on protecting kids when they're online. It offers advice on how to talk to kids about cyberbullying, online safety, and sexting. There are other topics that contain valuable information and help.

https://www.mentalhealth.gov/talk/parents-caregivers Here, they offer help for parents and caregivers about looking for signs of impaired mental health in kids. They also give information on supporting and getting help for children.

https://www.girlshealth.gov/bullying/school/index. html This website seems focused on talking directly to older kids, giving information about bullies, how to take action, and when to talk to teachers or adults in authority.

https://www.cdc.gov/healthyschools/bam/nutrition/ nutrition-facts-label.htm Here, you can get information on how to read nutrition labels, learn about how to improve your overall health through diet and physical activity.

About the Author

A nthony Montgomery was born and raised in the projects in Bronx, New York. He was "born into" the gang life, participated, became a leader, then readjusted his priorities. He now works toward encouraging youth to find productive outlets for their time and energy, educating people about bullying, in all its forms, and stopping violence through helping people treat each other. He is a proponent of spreading realization on the results of how words affect people, how hurtful interaction, picking on people, hurtful teasing, and abuse in all forms. He believes we can all be better people if we learn, teach, and work to improve our situations in life.

CPSIA information can be obtained
at www.ICGtesting.com
Printed in the USA
LVHW040703280720
661633LV00004B/362